DINO MANIA!

An Epic Battle of Dinosaur Facts

DINOSAURS GO HEAD-TO-HEAD!

Record Setters, All-Stars, and More Matchups

BY BECKY BAINES

Illustrated by Daniel Paul

PAW PRINTS
PUBLISHING

TABLE OF CONTENTS

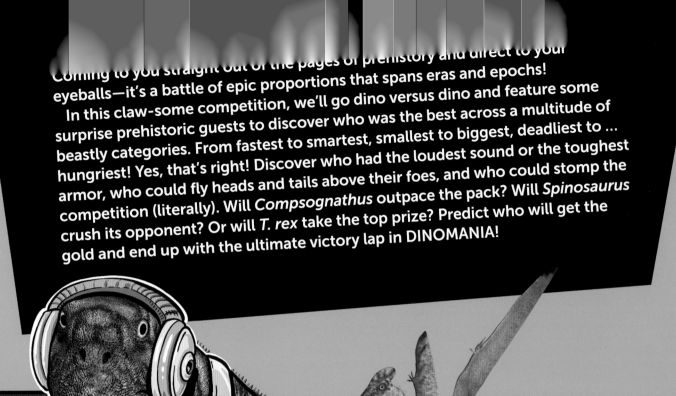

Coming to you straight out of the pages of prehistory and direct to your eyeballs—it's a battle of epic proportions that spans eras and epochs!

In this claw-some competition, we'll go dino versus dino and feature some surprise prehistoric guests to discover who was the best across a multitude of beastly categories. From fastest to smartest, smallest to biggest, deadliest to ... hungriest! Yes, that's right! Discover who had the loudest sound or the toughest armor, who could fly heads and tails above their foes, and who could stomp the competition (literally). Will *Compsognathus* outpace the pack? Will *Spinosaurus* crush its opponent? Or will *T. rex* take the top prize? Predict who will get the gold and end up with the ultimate victory lap in DINOMANIA!

DINO MANIA!

LIVE ACTION

Taking One for the Team

In this book, you'll discover a lot that dinosaurs could do: climb, swoop, soar, and even dance! But this Mesozoic competition isn't just about getting the gold; it's all about survival. To be number one meant making it another day in a dino-eat-dino world. Competition is a little different for us humans. It helps us build confidence, work toward goals, and strive to be our best. (Plus, we get cool trophies.) Sometimes you have to think more like a sauropod and less like *Spinosaurus*—instead of gnashing your teeth and looking out for number one, sometimes it's about looking out for each other. Being a team player beats being a sole winner any day!

ON YOUR MARK, GET SET, GO!

Could you outrun *Stegosaurus*? Considering they could run a mile (1.6 km) in six minutes, you might have a tough time keeping up! But compared to some of these rapid reptiles, *Stegosaurus* doesn't even begin to stack up. Check out the chart below to see which dino speed racers were crossing the finish line first.

1st

^ **Gallimimus**
50 miles an hour (80 km/h)

Clocking in with bursts of speed up to 50 miles an hour (80 km/h), *Gallimimus*, which means "chicken mimic," closely resembled an ostrich. This lean and agile omnivore was one of (if not *the*) fastest dinosaurs ever.

2nd

^ **Nanotyrannus**
Possibly up to 50 miles an hour (80 km/h)

Scientists long debated whether *Nanotyrannus* was just a juvenile *T. rex* or its own separate species, but fossils that surfaced in January 2024 settled the debate: This tiny tyrant was the real deal. And there's no denying it was fast—possibly running at max speeds of 50 miles an hour (80 km/h). It's often called the cheetah of the dinosaur world.

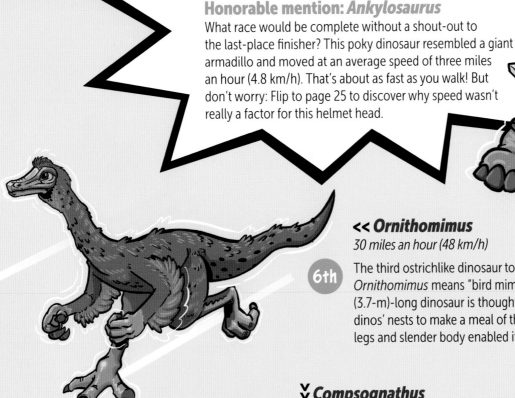

Honorable mention: *Ankylosaurus*

What race would be complete without a shout-out to the last-place finisher? This poky dinosaur resembled a giant armadillo and moved at an average speed of three miles an hour (4.8 km/h). That's about as fast as you walk! But don't worry: Flip to page 25 to discover why speed wasn't really a factor for this helmet head.

<< *Ornithomimus*

30 miles an hour (48 km/h)

6th The third ostrichlike dinosaur to grace the track, *Ornithomimus* means "bird mimic." This 12-foot (3.7-m)-long dinosaur is thought to have raided other dinos' nests to make a meal of their eggs. Its long back legs and slender body enabled it to make a fast getaway.

˅ *Compsognathus*

40 miles an hour (64 km/h)

Roughly the size of a chicken, this pint-size predator packs powerful speeds for its size. That quickness would have come in handy for chasing hard-to-catch prey. Scientists know *Compsognathus* was able to score some other speedsters for dinner—one skeleton was discovered with a fossilized lizard in its stomach.

5th

^ *Troodon*

30–40 miles an hour (48–64 km/h)

This birdlike, predatory dino boasts many abilities, including being the smartest of all dinosaurs (see page 11). But its razor-sharp teeth and its zooming speeds are what made it such a formidable foe!

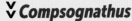

4th

3rd

^ *Struthiomimus*

30–50 miles an hour (48–80 km/h)

This *Gallimimus* look-alike's name actually translates to "ostrich mimic," and you might be fooled seeing the two side by side. They also rival each other in speed, but experts think *Struthiomimus* could clock only 50-mile-an-hour (80-km/h) speeds for short sprints, so it lags just behind its competition.

Determining Speed

How do we know how fast these dinos were? Well, the science isn't exact, but some researchers have developed a method to determine speed by studying leg fossils. First, they measure the upper leg bone (femur), which helps them understand the weight and size of the species. Then they use this to estimate how long the lower leg bone (tibia) should have been. In nature, the fastest animals have longer lower leg bones than upper leg bones because they are more adapted for running. Using this knowledge and the leg bone measurements, scientists determine what they call a cursorial limb proportion (CLP) score. First the scientists measure the actual lower leg bone. The higher the number is from where they expected it to be, the higher the CLP score— and the faster the animal. If the number is lower, the animal will receive a

DINO OLYMPICS

With roughly 700 species of dinosaurs discovered (and certainly many more that remain a mystery), there's no shortage of special skills in this very diverse group of animals. But have you ever wondered which dinosaurs would have won gold in their very own Dinosaur Olympics? OK, maybe not. But now you can! Check out these four contenders for top prize that could be crowned most epic of their epoch!

FIGURE SKATING

Tyrannosaurus rex

It's hard to believe an animal that could have weighed more than 30,000 pounds (13,608 kg) was anything but clumsy! But scientists think this prehistoric powerhouse possessed a secret skill that helped it hunt and claim gold in fictional figure skating: the incredible ability to twirl! Compared with other thundering theropods—the dominant predators of the Cretaceous—the body shape and massive muscles of *T. rex* enabled this dino to turn with great force, faster than many other predators. Combine that with terrifying teeth, supersharp senses, and stupendous speed, and you've got a seriously killer triple lutz!

BRRR! THE WATER IS CHILLY TODAY.

SWIMMING

Spinosaurus

Thinking of going for a swim during the age of the dinosaurs? Believe it or not, prehistoric sharks might have been the least of your concerns. When you see a telltale fin coming your way, just hope it's not *Spinosaurus*—captain of the scary, scaly swim team! This crocodile-jawed beast was semiaquatic, spending much of its time in the water hunting fish. But whether it was actually a good swimmer is up for debate: Some scientists argue the bone density of *Spinosaurus* suggests its swimming was mediocre at best. It likely waded in shallow waters waiting for its next unlucky meal to come along.

HIGH JUMP

Velociraptor

Weighing about the same as a modern-day turkey, *Velociraptor* was a pint-size predator that was not to be messed with. By studying the bones of *Velociraptor* legs and tails, researchers think this species was a master of the high jump. It could speedily spring up to 10 feet (3 m) in the air and take down prey like lizards, mammals, and baby dinos. Speed, strength, and a sickle-shaped claw? Just be glad it jumped its last jump around 70 million years ago!

GYMNASTICS

Mamenchisaurus

Calling *Mamenchisaurus* the Simone Biles of the Mesozoic may be a bit of a stretch, but so was everything about this hefty herbivore. A whopping half of its body was made up of just its neck, which could have been up to 50 feet (15 m) long. Like its modern-day doppelgänger, the giraffe, *Mamenchisaurus* went to great lengths to rip leaves off of the tippy-tops of trees. Unlike giraffes, its neck was longer than a school bus! Though *Mamenchisaurus* may not have mastered a forward roll, there's no denying it could stretch out longer than any creature in history. Stand atop the podium, *Mamenchisaurus*!

A dancing dino? You betcha! Scientists uncovered evidence that some dinosaurs used fancy footwork to attract a mate—just like some birds.

BEST IN CLASS

Welcome to the smackdown of the century! In the right corner, weighing in at a combined 225 tons (204 t), we have the towering titanosaurs, the colossal creatures of the Cretaceous, the SUPER SAUROPODS! And in the left corner, tipping the scales at around four pounds (1.8 kg), we have a group of itty-bitties so small that if you blink you might miss them—it's the TINY DINIES!

TINY DINIES

Aquilops

What's the size of a bunny with the face of an eagle, the frill of a lizard, and beak of a toucan? No, it's not a science experiment gone wrong—it's *Aquilops*! Scientists study fossils of its lemon-size skull to unlock secrets of its relatives, the Ceratopsian family. These were horned herbivores, which also include *Protoceratops* and *Diabloceratops*. How do they know this three pound (1.4 kg) cutie isn't just a baby dino? By studying its teeth! Much like tree rings, teeth have growth lines that can be used to tell how old an animal is.

Archaeopteryx

Archaeopteryx has a pretty cool claim to fame: It was the first feathered fossil ever discovered. This birdlike dino was discovered in 1861, but scientists are still uncovering its secrets. For a long time, they thought it was a glider like *Microraptor*, but recent studies suggest *Archaeopteryx* could fly in short bursts, taking off from ground level with a running start. And at around two pounds (0.9 kg), its small size helped it catch some serious air.

Microraptor

Covered in iridescent feathers like a peacock, this small show-off couldn't fly, but instead used tiny talons to scale trees and then spread its wings to glide through the air to snap up insects for dinner. Maxing out at around two pounds (0.9 kg) and one foot (0.3 m) tall, *Microraptor*'s light-as-a-feather size and birdlike qualities furthered the mounting evidence that birds are directly descended from dinosaurs.

Microraptor was so small, an adult human could have held it in their hand!

SUPER SAUROPODS

Argentinosaurus

This huge herbivore is often recognized as the largest land animal to ever exist. Rivaling the weight of a modern-day blue whale, this behemoth beast could have weighed up to 90 tons (82 t) and measured up to 115 feet (35 m) long. Paleontologists have never unearthed a full skeleton of *Argentinosaurus* (or any titanosaur for that matter), so they estimate based on the size of fossils and by creating digital reconstructions. Was *Argentinosaurus* the largest dino ever? *Patagotitan mayorum* might have something to say about that ...

Some sauropods were so big because they didn't stop growing until they were around 30 years old!

Patagotitan mayorum

This titanosaur's size was close to that of *Argentinosaurus*, with some scientists speculating that it could have been bigger. But the best guess for this beast is an average weight of 70 tons (64 t) and length of 122 feet (37 m). Nice try, *Patagotitan*, but *Argentinosaurus* has got you beat!

Dreadnoughtus

This colossal creature's name may send a shiver down your spine. Named after a type of battleship, *Dreadnoughtus* roughly translates to "fear nothing." That's because this sauropod was so huge and had such an incredibly powerful tail that it likely had nothing to fear. Coming in at a respectable 65 tons (59 t) and 85 feet (26 m) in length, *Dreadnoughtus* weighed more than 20 pickup trucks.

BATTLE OF THE BRAINS

To say dinosaurs were birdbrained is anything but an insult. After all, most scientists agree that today's birds are directly descended from dinos! And birds are among the most intelligent animals. So is it any surprise that, in some cases, the apple didn't fall too far from the tree? Follow the bracket below to see which extinct egghead would make it to the head of the class!

ROUND 1

Tyrannosaurus rex VS. **Allosaurus**

Allosaurus and *T. rex* may look similar, but these two members of the theropod family had some distinct differences. First, *Allosaurus* lived in the late Jurassic period—about 80 million years before *T. rex*. It was also smaller and more of an opportunistic hunter and scavenger than a skilled stalker of prey, and it had a smaller brain. With the size advantage and smarts on its side, *T. rex* would have had this matchup in the bag!

 WINNER! **T. rex**

Ornithomimus VS. **Deinonychus**

Ornithomimus means "bird mimic," and it's no wonder because it looks remarkably similar to the long-legged featherheads of today. And like some of today's birds, it was one smart cookie! But *Ornithomimus* couldn't outsmart *Deinonychus*, a powerhouse predator with a lethal "killing claw" on each foot. Scientists rank this clever carnivore as both one of the fastest and most intelligent dinosaurs.

WINNER! **Deinonychus**

Velociraptor VS. **Troodon**

A big brain and keen senses go hand in hand, and *Troodon* and *Velociraptor* rank high for both. They were both strong hunters, boasting the same clawed toe, sharp teeth, and powerful night vision that gave them an edge against prey. But *Troodon* was so smart that some scientists believe it would have evolved to have even more advanced intelligence if not for that pesky mass extinction.

 WINNER! **Troodon**

Compsognathus VS. **Oviraptor**

Scientists once thought *Oviraptor* was the criminal of the Cretaceous. With a name that translates to "egg thief," this daring dino was thought to use its intelligence for dastardly deeds. But evidence proves *Oviraptor* was not an egg stealer, but an egg nurturer, with brainy survival instincts. But with a bigger brain and seriously smart hunting skills, *Compsognathus* takes home the prize! Scientists think this mini menace may have teamed up with others of its species to take down larger prey. Talk about a family meal deal!

WINNER! **Compsognathus**

EQ-scuse Me?

The encephalization quotient (EQ)—which determines the size of an animal's brain compared to its body size—gives scientists a very good understanding of an animal's capacity for intelligence. But that's not the only factor to be considered. Bottlenose dolphins, some of the smartest creatures on the planet, have an EQ of 5.6, and humans have an EQ of up to 7.8. Does that mean dolphins are almost as smart as humans? Not necessarily. There's also the intelligence quotient (IQ) which measures a person's ability to reason. Though scientists can measure brain size, there's no one-size-fits-all IQ test. Recent studies also show that more factors are at play, like brain structure and the number of neurons. So humans' number one spot is secure—for now!

ROUND 2

Tyrannosaurus rex   Deinonychus

T. rex takes top honors in many record-breaking categories, but when it comes to smarts, it's no match for the dromaeosaurids. This remarkable group of raptors (which includes *Deinonychus* and *Velociraptor*) may come from the same order as *T. rex* (theropods), but they had bigger brains compared to body size and could outwit most other creatures of the day.

 **Deinonychus**

Troodon   Compsognathus

In a battle of wits, *Troodon* would have beaten *Compsognathus* by a feather. *Compsognathus* was a hunter of small, swift animals, which means it needed both speed and smarts. But brain size doesn't lie, and *Troodon* may be the only dino out there who could defeat a dromaeosaurid.

 Troodon

ROUND 3

Deinonychus   Troodon

This matchup is so close it would probably need a photo finish, so we have to look at the science. *Troodon* had an EQ of 5.8, leading most scientists to conclude that it was the smartest of all the dinosaurs discovered to date. With an EQ between 5.5 and 5.8, *Deinonychus* puts in a respectable performance, but just misses the top spot.

WINNER!

Troodon

MONSTER MATCHUPS!

From spooky to downright terrifying, see some of the most frightening prehistoric creatures go head-to-head in these scare-your-pants-off categories!

Jeholopterus

SPOOKIEST SPECIES

Pegomastax

What do you get if you cross a dinosaur, a porcupine, and a parrot with fearsome fangs? *Pegomastax*, the "fanged vampire parrot." This pint-size nightmare crept across prehistoric Africa, no doubt out-weirding even the most curious creatures of the Jurassic. But top honor in this category actually goes to a hotly debated pterosaur called *Jeholopterus*, which looked like a cross between a bird, a bat, and a turtle. Some scientists think it may have been a bloodsucking species that attached itself to the bellies of large dinos to feed like vampire bats!

BEST IN BITE

T. rex

When it comes to gigantic jaws, there's no shortage of dinosaurs with terrifying teeth. But when it comes to bite strength, *T. rex* packed a powerful punch. Though everything about *T. rex* made it a certified killing machine, its deadly bite force sealed the deal. When those jaws came crashing down, they did so with 12,800 pounds (5,806 kg) of force. But that's not quite as impressive as *Sarcosuchus* (also known as SuperCroc). This ancient crocodile snacked on dinosaurs for lunch. With a bite force of roughly 18,000 pounds (8,165 kg), this croc rocks this matchup!

CLAW-SOME CREATURES

Therizinosaurus

Utahraptor

Many dinos boasted fearsome claws that they used for digging, scratching, thrashing, and shredding. But if prehistoric nail salons existed, *Therizinosaurus* and *Utahraptor* would be VIPs. *Utahraptor* could deliver a lethal blow to enemies in just one swoop, which came in handy in a dino-eat-dino world. But the incredible claws of *Therizinosaurus* take the cake. Although scientists believe they were too flimsy to use for defense, the claws measured an amazing 3.2 feet (1 m), leaving the measly nine-inch (23-cm) nails of *Utahraptor* in the dust!

NIGHT CRAWLERS

Hunting in the dark has a lot of perks, including less competition for prey and less exposure to predators. Two dinos were night-stalking specialists: *Haplocheirus sollers* and *Shuvuuia deserti.* By studying the skeletons of these tiny theropods, experts have noticed the similarities in eye socket structure to modern-day birds with superior night vision, like owls. Though it wasn't uncommon for smaller carnivores to hunt at night, the facial structures of this duo suggest they were pros. But when it comes to another key hunting adaptation, superior hearing, *Shuvuuia* is the winner of this nocturnal knockout.

Shuvuuia deserti

Haplocheirus sollers

Sarcosuchus

Dracorex hogwartsia, a spiky-horned dragon dino, looked like something straight out of the wizarding world. But scientists disagree whether it was a real species, or actually just a juvenile *Pachycephalosaurus*.

SCARY SWIM TEAM

If the idea of swimming with the fishes gives you the heebie-jeebies today, you wouldn't want to take a dip during prehistoric days. It's time for a deeper dive to discover the ferocious creatures lurking in the depths. Check out these four competitors for the scariest swim meet ever!

AHH!

Mosasaurs

Measuring a maximum of 56 feet (17 m) in length, mosasaurs were some of the most fearsome creatures prowling the ocean. That's because they would dine on anything that dashed their way. An ancestor of today's snakes, mosasaurs were an incredibly diverse species. Some likely lurked in more shallow waters, crunching on shellfish with their curved teeth. Others used their long snakelike bodies and hinged jaws to chase faster prey into deeper waters—snapping up anything from fish to sharks to other mosasaurs and swallowing them nearly whole!

All types of wicked wonders have been lurking beneath the waves for a long time. During the Silurian age (about 443 million years ago), sea-dwelling scorpions—arthropods (like crabs and spiders) the size of dogs—with sharp claws for catching prey crawled across the sandy bottom.

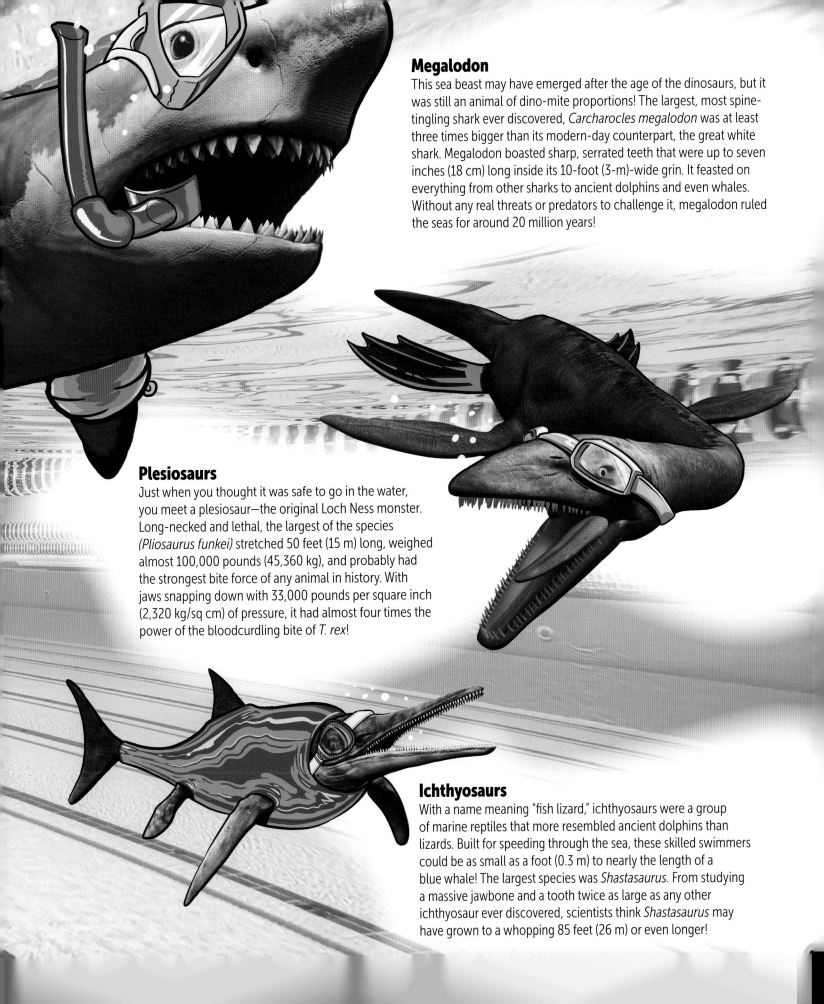

Megalodon

This sea beast may have emerged after the age of the dinosaurs, but it was still an animal of dino-mite proportions! The largest, most spine-tingling shark ever discovered, *Carcharocles megalodon* was at least three times bigger than its modern-day counterpart, the great white shark. Megalodon boasted sharp, serrated teeth that were up to seven inches (18 cm) long inside its 10-foot (3-m)-wide grin. It feasted on everything from other sharks to ancient dolphins and even whales. Without any real threats or predators to challenge it, megalodon ruled the seas for around 20 million years!

Plesiosaurs

Just when you thought it was safe to go in the water, you meet a plesiosaur—the original Loch Ness monster. Long-necked and lethal, the largest of the species (*Pliosaurus funkei*) stretched 50 feet (15 m) long, weighed almost 100,000 pounds (45,360 kg), and probably had the strongest bite force of any animal in history. With jaws snapping down with 33,000 pounds per square inch (2,320 kg/sq cm) of pressure, it had almost four times the power of the bloodcurdling bite of *T. rex*!

Ichthyosaurs

With a name meaning "fish lizard," ichthyosaurs were a group of marine reptiles that more resembled ancient dolphins than lizards. Built for speeding through the sea, these skilled swimmers could be as small as a foot (0.3 m) to nearly the length of a blue whale! The largest species was *Shastasaurus*. From studying a massive jawbone and a tooth twice as large as any other ichthyosaur ever discovered, scientists think *Shastasaurus* may have grown to a whopping 85 feet (26 m) or even longer!

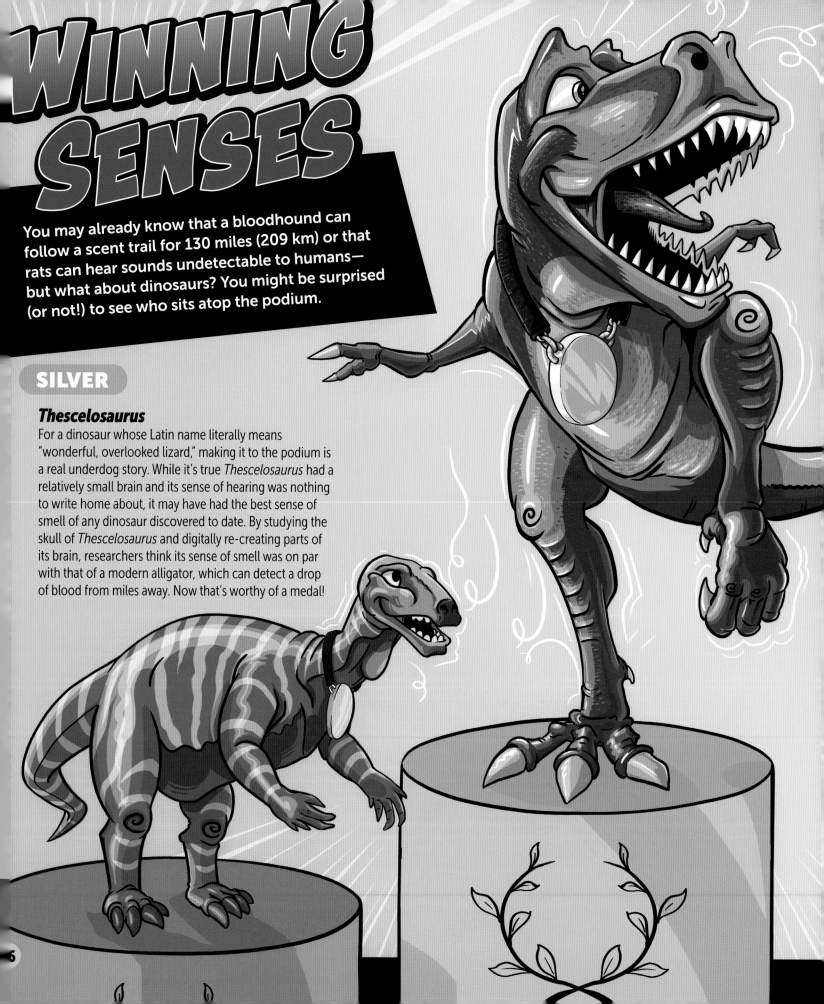

WINNING SENSES

You may already know that a bloodhound can follow a scent trail for 130 miles (209 km) or that rats can hear sounds undetectable to humans—but what about dinosaurs? You might be surprised (or not!) to see who sits atop the podium.

SILVER

Thescelosaurus

For a dinosaur whose Latin name literally means "wonderful, overlooked lizard," making it to the podium is a real underdog story. While it's true *Thescelosaurus* had a relatively small brain and its sense of hearing was nothing to write home about, it may have had the best sense of smell of any dinosaur discovered to date. By studying the skull of *Thescelosaurus* and digitally re-creating parts of its brain, researchers think its sense of smell was on par with that of a modern alligator, which can detect a drop of blood from miles away. Now that's worthy of a medal!

Tyrannosaurus rex

Taking on *T. rex* for any top spot is just not really a fair fight. As for sensational senses, the terrible tyrant had it all: hearing, smell, and vision! With eyeballs the size of oranges and probably an ability to see colors on the ultraviolet spectrum, *T. rex* used its binocular vision to pinpoint prey in dense tree-filled landscapes. It also had enlarged olfactory bulbs (smelling parts) in its brain, and elongated bones in its ears that made its hearing extra sensitive. Combine those with a high level of intelligence, crushing jaw strength, and speed? No wonder it's always the MVP!

Triceratops

Eye Spy

Dinosaurs had different types of vision depending on their needs. Predators, like *Troodon* and *T. rex*, had forward-facing eyeballs and binocular vision, which is helpful when determining the location of an object. Humans have binocular vision too! You can test it out by closing one eye while looking at an object—then close the other eye, and look at the same object. You'll notice the position of the object changes slightly in your field of vision. Your brain combines the images received from both eyes to determine the distance of the object. Prey animals, like *Apatosaurus* or *Triceratops*, had peripheral vision. With eyes located on either side of their head rather than forward-facing, they could see all around them at any given time. This gave them the advantage when scouting the landscape for potential danger.

Llukalkan

This recently studied species of abelisaurid theropod (the ones with the really tiny arms) was likely the largest predator roaming modern-day Argentina 80 million years ago. Its name means "the one who causes fear" for a reason: If being a 16-foot (4.9-m)-long cousin of *T. rex* wasn't enough to strike terror in the hearts of potential prey, its highly developed sense of hearing might be. By examining its skull, scientists discovered the area that perceives sound adapted differently than in its carnivorous cohorts, which would have given it a leg up while hunting.

SETTING THE RECORD

From mega jaws and colossal claws to epic events and weird wonders, the race to first place is always about setting a personal best. Read below to dig up all the dino dirt on these record-breaking relics and more!

MOST EXPENSIVE FOSSIL

Stan

The most complete *T. rex* fossil ever found, Stan—measuring 13 feet (4 m) tall and 40 feet (12 m) long—was the subject of a lot of controversy when it was sold at a private auction in 2020. A bidder paid nearly $32 million for the fantastic find. People feared the sale of an important specimen to a personal collector meant it would be lost to science forever, but they were relieved to learn the purchaser was a natural history museum in Abu Dhabi, the capital of the United Arab Emirates—and that researchers will still have access to uncover Stan's secrets.

BIGGEST DINOSAUR DISCOVERED

Máximo

A sheepherder on a ranch in Argentina was minding his flock when he stumbled across what would become the biggest dino discovery in the history of the world. Paleontologists spent five years excavating 200 bones of *Patagotitan mayorum,* a titanosaur. While they believe the fossils at the site actually came from at least six different titanosaurs, experts were able to use the parts to create a replica skeleton with extreme accuracy. Now they have three full replicas, one of which resides at the Field Museum in Chicago U.S.A. At 122 feet (37 m) long, Máximo is a lifelike dinosaur skeleton that scientists had to piece together like a giant jigsaw puzzle to fit it inside the building!

BEST-PRESERVED FOSSIL

Borealopelta

A fossil of this 18-foot (5.5-m)-long species of ankylosaur, unearthed in modern-day Canada, featured visible armor. This super-rare find gave scientists the opportunity to learn about dinosaurs like never before! The last meal of this *Borealopelta* was also still in its stomach, fossilized along with the rest of its body. Researchers believe this specimen, having roamed Earth about 110 million years ago, sank in the mud at the bottom of the sea when it died, creating a perfect preservation chamber.

BIGGEST MURDER MYSTERY

Utah's Dino Fossil Pit

For years, scientists have been trying to crack the case of what happened 148 million years ago when 74 individual dinosaurs, most of them predators, became trapped in the world's densest dino fossil pit ever uncovered. Paleontologists have discovered in the Cleveland-Lloyd Dinosaur Quarry at least 15,000 bones belonging to *Stegosaurus, Allosaurus,* and more with bite marks indicating they tried eating each other in a desperate last-ditch attempt for survival. Theories range from poisoned water to a muddy pond, but so far there has been no final word on what caused their ultimate demise.

BONUS ROUND!

BIGGEST DINO EXTINCTION EVENT

K–Pg Extinction

The asteroid impact that ended the reign of the dinosaurs wasn't the first mass extinction to hit planet Earth, but it was a doozy. The blast and its aftereffects wiped out roughly 75 to 80 percent of all life that existed at that time, including all the non-avian dinosaurs and marine reptiles. But the impact itself didn't cause their untimely death; it was the abrupt shift in climate that most species could not survive. And if that didn't do it, the massive cloud of dust that suffocated the planet was probably the kicker.

MEGA MEALS

Come one, come all—dine with dinos at the all-you-can-eat buffet! In this prehistoric beast feast, it's survival of the hungriest as the biggest dinosaurs had to supersize their meals to maintain their, well, supersize. Check out these awesome appetites to determine who would be crowned champion of this epic eating contest!

OM NOM NOM NOM

Allosaurus

These lean, mean, meat-eating machines had a variety of Jurassic creatures on their menus! Scientists think they snacked on huge sauropods like *Diplodocus* and *Apatosaurus*. But there's also evidence of puncture wounds from the sharp tail of a *Stegosaurus* in *Allosaurus* fossils, meaning they didn't shy away from armored animals. Researchers also uncovered a pit that had fossils of *Allosaurus* with bite marks from other *Allosaurus*. In other words, when food was tough to find, they didn't hesitate to eat their own kind!

Spinosaurus

The science around the eating habits of this ancient anomaly has been the subject of debate. Scientists made a breakthrough when they determined that *Spinosaurus* was a semiaquatic dino—using its long, sharp teeth and crocodile-like jaws to ambush prehistoric fish and large sharks! But other evidence suggests it was more of a wader—and may have also dined on land-dwelling dinos like other mega carnivores of the day. What surprises does *Spinosaurus* have left in store? Only time will tell. But one thing we do know: Weighing as much as a whopping 22 tons (20 t), this beast could feast!

With all munching and no brushing, can you imagine how stinky dino breath must have been? Now you don't have to! At Chicago's Field Museum, simply press a button and you too can get a whiff of fresh *T. rex* breath!

Giganotosaurus

When it comes to king of the prehistoric jungle, *Giganotosaurus* ruled the roost long before *T. rex* ever came along. *Giganotosaurus* clomped around the early Cretaceous eating none other than giants like *Argentinosaurus*. But how could anything wrap its jaws around a dinosaur the size of a house? *Giganotosaurus* was more of a slicer than a chomper. It typically wounded its prey rather than taking full bites. Plus, it may have hunted in packs. And what's more terrifying than a carnivore bigger than *T. rex*? A whole pack of them. That's one way to score a meal fit for a king!

Argentinosaurus

Would you believe that the largest dinosaur to walk the Earth was actually an herbivore? Stretching longer than a basketball court, *Argentinosaurus* had to eat a ton to nourish its massive body with just plant matter. Literally. Scientists use calculations based on what we know from today's largest land animal (and fellow herbivore), the African elephant, to determine the diet of *Argentinosaurus*. They figure the number would be around 1,880 pounds (853 kg) of plants a day to keep up its fit, full figure.

FANTASTIC FLIERS

Two key features help animals take flight: wings and light or hollow bones. And even though plenty of dinos boasted both, evidence shows avian dinosaurs were actually better at climbing and gliding than swooping and soaring. So who were the frequent fliers booking miles of airtime across prehistoric skies? It was a different group entirely! Meet the non-dinosaur reptiles that dominated early flight: pterosaurs.

Pterodactylus

Perhaps the most famous pterosaur, *Pterodactylus* caused confusion from the start. When an Italian scientist first discovered the fossil in 1784, he thought it was a marine animal with long fins, not wings. A naturalist suggested in the early 1800s that these were actually fossilized fliers instead of swimmers. Soon, he started calling them all "ptero-dactyles" and the nickname stuck around. But as science advanced and different kinds of pterosaurs were unearthed (about 150 in total), it was clear that *Pterodactylus* was just one of many. And with a modest wingspan of three feet (0.9 m), its name is definitely its claim to fame!

The largest pterosaurs could fly up to 400 miles (644 km) a day.

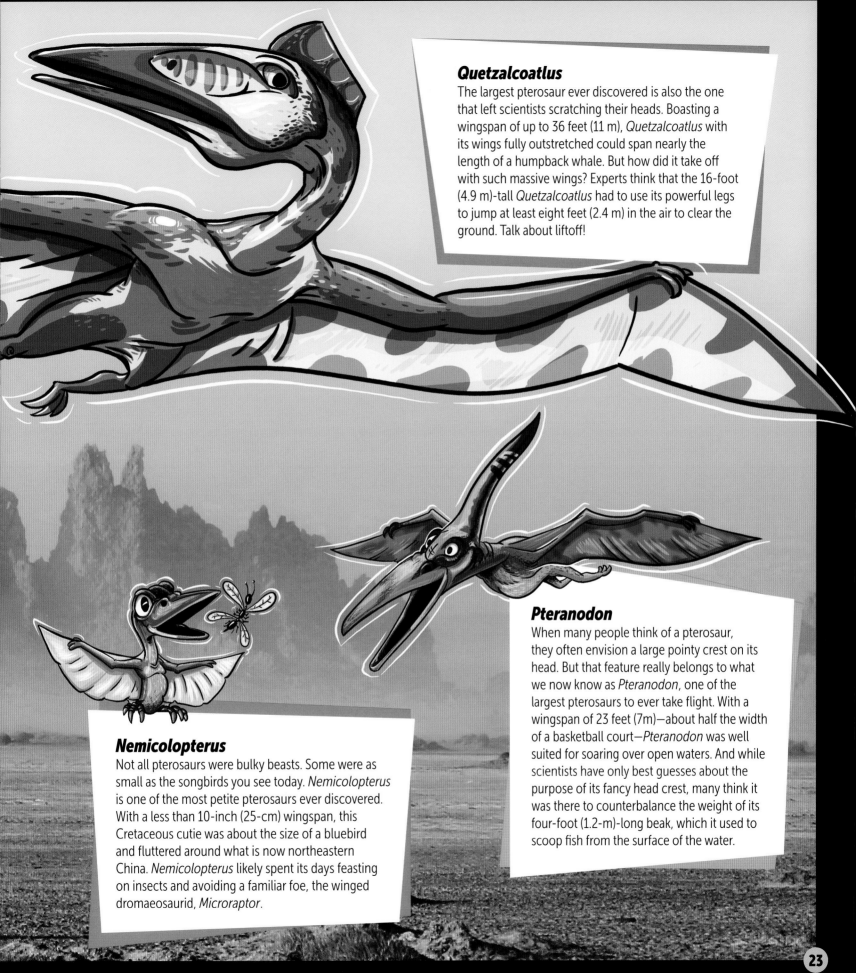

Quetzalcoatlus

The largest pterosaur ever discovered is also the one that left scientists scratching their heads. Boasting a wingspan of up to 36 feet (11 m), *Quetzalcoatlus* with its wings fully outstretched could span nearly the length of a humpback whale. But how did it take off with such massive wings? Experts think that the 16-foot (4.9 m)-tall *Quetzalcoatlus* had to use its powerful legs to jump at least eight feet (2.4 m) in the air to clear the ground. Talk about liftoff!

Pteranodon

When many people think of a pterosaur, they often envision a large pointy crest on its head. But that feature really belongs to what we now know as *Pteranodon*, one of the largest pterosaurs to ever take flight. With a wingspan of 23 feet (7m)—about half the width of a basketball court—*Pteranodon* was well suited for soaring over open waters. And while scientists have only best guesses about the purpose of its fancy head crest, many think it was there to counterbalance the weight of its four-foot (1.2-m)-long beak, which it used to scoop fish from the surface of the water.

Nemicolopterus

Not all pterosaurs were bulky beasts. Some were as small as the songbirds you see today. *Nemicolopterus* is one of the most petite pterosaurs ever discovered. With a less than 10-inch (25-cm) wingspan, this Cretaceous cutie was about the size of a bluebird and fluttered around what is now northeastern China. *Nemicolopterus* likely spent its days feasting on insects and avoiding a familiar foe, the winged dromaeosaurid, *Microraptor*.

SUPER DINO MATCHUPS!

While dinosaurs may not have worn capes, they definitely had some superpowers. From armor to smell and more, see dinos go head-to-head in these power-packed categories.

LOUDEST DINOSAUR

We may not have recordings of what dinos actually sounded like, but by comparing fossil findings, similarities in modern-day animals, and general knowledge of how sounds are made, scientists are starting to find out. And according to experts, the movies get it wrong. *T. rex* wasn't a roarer like you see on the screen: It was a closed-mouth vocalizer like birds and crocodiles. It probably had a softer sound in the form of coos and low-pitched rumbles. The loudest dinosaurs weren't roarers either: Some hadrosaurs, or duck-billed dinosaurs, had large crests on their heads that may have been used somewhat like an instrument. By re-creating their skeletons and experimenting with digital vocal cords, experts think these guys could make loud "toot-toot" sounds at different levels and frequencies.

Parasaurolophus

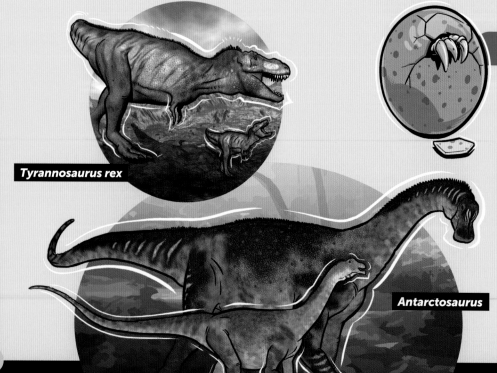

Tyrannosaurus rex

Antarctosaurus

BIGGEST BABY

It only makes sense to think the biggest dinosaurs also had the biggest babies. But did soaring sauropods give birth to 10-foot (3-m) infants? Not quite. In fact, sauropod hatchlings, even massive titanosaurs, weighed only a measly six to eight pounds (2.7 to 3.6 kg). That's not much bigger than a human baby. No wonder it took 20 years to reach the size of a school bus! Recent studies reveal the other end of the scale: Tyrannosaurs had the largest hatchlings discovered to date. The baby would have been about three feet (0.9 m) tall when it emerged from its egg and looked remarkably like the adult-size version of itself. Now that's *eggs*traordinary!

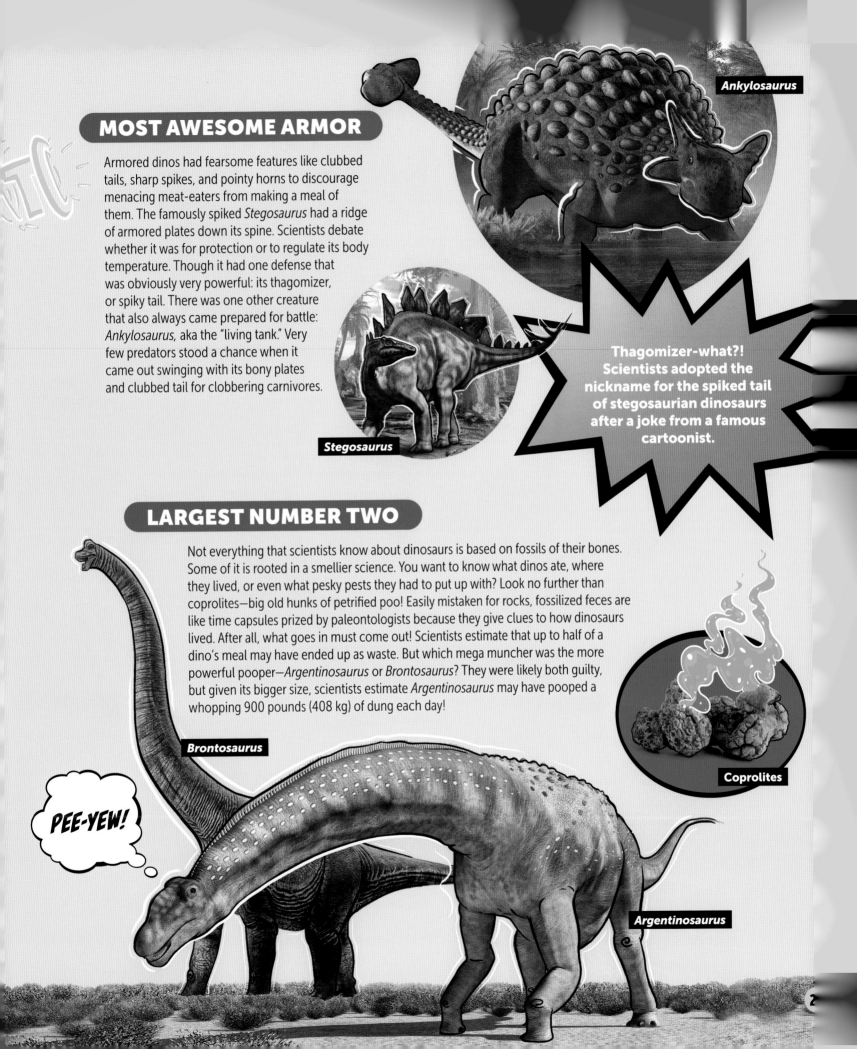

MOST AWESOME ARMOR

Armored dinos had fearsome features like clubbed tails, sharp spikes, and pointy horns to discourage menacing meat-eaters from making a meal of them. The famously spiked *Stegosaurus* had a ridge of armored plates down its spine. Scientists debate whether it was for protection or to regulate its body temperature. Though it had one defense that was obviously very powerful: its thagomizer, or spiky tail. There was one other creature that also always came prepared for battle: *Ankylosaurus,* aka the "living tank." Very few predators stood a chance when it came out swinging with its bony plates and clubbed tail for clobbering carnivores.

Ankylosaurus

Stegosaurus

Thagomizer-what?! Scientists adopted the nickname for the spiked tail of stegosaurian dinosaurs after a joke from a famous cartoonist.

LARGEST NUMBER TWO

Not everything that scientists know about dinosaurs is based on fossils of their bones. Some of it is rooted in a smellier science. You want to know what dinos ate, where they lived, or even what pesky pests they had to put up with? Look no further than coprolites—big old hunks of petrified poo! Easily mistaken for rocks, fossilized feces are like time capsules prized by paleontologists because they give clues to how dinosaurs lived. After all, what goes in must come out! Scientists estimate that up to half of a dino's meal may have ended up as waste. But which mega muncher was the more powerful pooper—*Argentinosaurus* or *Brontosaurus*? They were likely both guilty, but given its bigger size, scientists estimate *Argentinosaurus* may have pooped a whopping 900 pounds (408 kg) of dung each day!

Coprolites

Brontosaurus

PEE-YEW!

Argentinosaurus

ODDBALL ALL-STARS

When it comes to ancient oddities, there's no shortage of dinosaurs with bizarre bragging rights! If you were fielding a far-out team of the feathered and ferocious, would these peculiar players make the cut?

Triceratops

Length: 30 feet (9 m)
Weight: Up to 16,000 pounds (7,257 kg)
Years Active: 70 million–65 million years ago
Claim to Fame: Heftiest Head

This herbivore whose name translates to "three-horned face" was probably a favorite meal of its Cretaceous companion, *T. rex*. But *Triceratops* wouldn't have been easy prey: With a large frilled head measuring up to seven feet (2 m) across, it used its harrowing horns and sizable skull to duel enemies. That's one hardy headbutt!

TRICERATOPS

CARNOTAURUS

Carnotaurus

Length: 26 feet (8 m)
Weight: Up to 3,000 pounds (1,360 kg)
Years Active: 71 million–69 million years ago
Claim to Fame: Teeny Tiny Arms

Poor *T. rex* gets a bad rap for its little arms, but it's got nothing on *Carnotaurus*! This "meat-eating bull" looks like a horrible, horned monster, but closer examination of its front appendages revealed two tiny foot-long (60 cm) limbs with no elbows! Scientists think they were vestigial features—meaning they were leftover traits from ancestors that no longer had use.

Nigersaurus
Length: 30 feet (9 m)
Weight: Up to 8,000 pounds (3,629 kg)
Years Active: 110 million years ago
Claim to Fame: Fastest Regrowing Teeth

With a head shaped like a vacuum cleaner and a hankering for plants, *Nigersaurus* has been called a "Mesozoic cow." *Nigersaurus* had something called "dental batteries," tightly packed columns of teeth. If one fell out, it had a backup waiting right behind it. Its mouth held as many as five replacements for every tooth at any given time, and it probably regrew them at a rate of once a month—the fastest of any dinosaur ever.

Megalosaurus
Length: 30 feet (9 m)
Weight: 2,000 pounds (907 kg)
Years Active: 176 million–161 million years ago
Claim to Fame: First Scientifically Described Dino Discovery

Imagine you're at the beach building a sandcastle and you unearth the body of an alien! That's what it may have been like for people throughout history who accidentally dug up dino bones. Explanations ranged from human giants to dragons to griffins and more. It wasn't until 1824 that William Buckland named a fossil *Megalosaurus*, or "great lizard." It took 20 more years, and two more discoveries—*Iguanodon* and *Hylaeosaurus*—for paleontologist Sir Richard Owen to dub the group Dinosauria.

Who's on First?

So we know the first dinosaur named, but how about the first dinosaur ever? That gets a lot more complicated. For decades, that honor was bestowed upon *Eoraptor*, a three-foot (0.9-m)-long dino that has caused a ton of confusion. At first, it was considered the first theropod, and then scientists reexamined the evidence and declared it a sauropod. Some wonder if it wasn't a to rock *Eoraptor* is even more recent: Experts think *Nyasasaurus*, an ancient archosaur, may have beat *Eoraptor* to the scene by about 10 million years! But don't put that crown on just yet. Some scientists believe it's possible that about 70 percent of dinosaur species remain undiscovered, so it may not be long before *Nyasasaurus* is stepping aside for another famous first!

BATTLE OF THE BRAWN

In a dino-eat-dino world, playing to strengths was the key to survival. Some dinos had terrifying teeth; others had horns and awesome armor. And while determining the deadliest dino isn't always about brute strength, it doesn't hurt! Check out these prehistoric powerhouses to determine the winner.

ROUND 1

 **Majungasaurus** VS. **Giganotosaurus**

Majungasaurus was a 23-foot (7-m)-long bloodthirsty theropod who meant business when hunting prehistoric prey. But it was also one of the slowest-growing carnivores, and young dinos were easier targets for fellow predators. Additionally, its super-stubby arms were pretty useless when it came to defending itself. Compared to *Giganotosaurus*, which grew to a whopping 47 feet (14 m) and had a unique slasher style of taking down massive prey, it's no toss-up.

 WINNER! Giganotosaurus

 **Ankylosaurus** VS. **Tyrannosaurus rex**

Ankylosaurus may have been one of the slowest dinosaurs, but it boasted the size, weight, and formidability of a military tank. If that wasn't enough to scare off foes, its huge clubbed tail just might. Studies have shown one whack from this wieldy weapon would have been enough to crush bones. But we're also talking *T. rex* here, perhaps the deadliest carnivore in history with the strongest bite strength of any dino. Experts think its jaws could easily have broken through *Ankylosaurus*'s weaker spots. *T. rex* takes the win!

WINNER! T. rex

  **Spinosaurus** VS. **Titanosaurs**

A slow herbivore versus a crocodile-jawed killing machine? This is where weighing more than 100 tons (91 t) had its perks, including the fact that some scientists are skeptical that even a deadly carnivore like *Spinosaurus* could have taken down a fully grown titanosaur on its own (dinos that dared try may have teamed up to take them on). But juvenile titanosaurs would have been a substantial snack for any predator. And even though *Spinosaurus* preferred seafood, it could have eaten a titanosaur if it wanted to, thus making it the winner!

WINNER! Spinosaurus

  **Triceratops** VS. **Velociraptor**

Three ranchers dug up what are now known as the "dueling dinos," a fossilized *Triceratops* and *T. rex* engaged in battle. Both died of their injuries and the discovery confirmed decades of theory: *Triceratops* was not to be messed with. But how would it fare against *Velociraptor*? At less than two feet (0.6 m) tall, you would think that *Triceratops* could stomp *Velociraptor* easily. But what *Velociraptor* lacked in size, it made up in smarts and a sickle-shaped claw—one it used to dig in to its prey and keep it from escaping. *Velociraptor* is the victor!

WINNER! Velociraptor

A showdown of *T. rex* and *Giganotosaurus* was depicted in the movie *Jurassic World Dominion*. Though *T. rex* took the win, it wasn't without a little help from a mega-clawed *Therizinosaurus*.

ROUND 2

Giganotosaurus   Tyrannosaurus rex

When comparing size and scale, *Giganotosaurus* and *T. rex* are pretty evenly matched, though *Giganotosaurus* had a slight edge. Their hunting styles, however, were totally different: *T. rex* used its jaws to crush while *Giganotosaurus* used its teeth to slice. But when it came to killer senses, *T. rex* was a fine-tuned meat-eating machine, and it would have used its keen eyesight, hearing, and sense of smell to claim victory over *Giganotosaurus*. *T. rex* moves on to the final round!

 **T. rex**

T. rex vs. Spinosaurus
This battle deserves a bigger breakdown. Turn the page to see who is declared the most epic dino of all!

Spinosaurus   Velociraptor

Prehistory's largest carnivore versus one of the smallest may seem like a no-brainer, but never underestimate the super-crafty *Velociraptor*. After all, in round 1 he took down *Triceratops*! Unfortunately for *Velociraptor*, *Spinosaurus* had a few things *Triceratops* didn't: a mega-massive body, long neck, wide jaws full of sharp cone-shaped teeth, and claws like knife blades. And while it primarily hunted in and around water, it was pretty dangerous on land, running almost as fast as *T. rex*. *Spinosaurus* heads to the final round!

 **Spinosaurus**

WHO WOULD WIN?

SPINOSAURUS VS. T. REX

matchup of these muscly meatheads would be a clash of epic proportions—literally. Both colossal carnivores were easily the most dangerous dinos to rule their terrain. But *Spinosaurus*, which lived in modern-day North Africa, went extinct about 30 million years before *T. rex*, a resident of modern-day North America, even entered the picture. So though it's fun to imagine, a *Spino-T. rex* headline event never drew crowds from all over the Cretaceous. But if it had, who would have taken the title?

Supersize

There's no denying *Spinosaurus* had size on its side. Weighing between 12 and 22 tons (11 and 20 t), this behemoth bully was as long as two fire trucks end to end. The school bus-length frame of *T. rex* was a bit more compact, but still not exactly something you'd want chasing you for dinner! *Spinosaurus* also had a longer, lengthier body with a small head and crocodile-like mouth.

On the Hunt

While *Spinosaurus* could sprint up to 15 miles an hour (24 km/h), it preferred a watery hunting ground. The huge sail on its back, dense bones, and fleshy tail made it a great underwater eating machine, though it's possible it just ambushed dinosaurs headed to the water's edge for a drink. Unlike *Spinosaurus, T. rex* had long, muscular legs, perfect for chasing, and a huge head with massive jaws and teeth. It could run in bursts of up to 20 miles an hour (32 km/h) and had a bite force that could break through some of the toughest dino defenses. But what *T. rex* really had going for it was laser-sharp senses. Reigning champ in almost all categories, *T. rex* was a lean, mean killing machine. It also had a bigger brain than *Spinosaurus* and was able to zero in on other dinosaurs' weak spots to hit them where it hurt.

WINNER!

Terrifying Teeth

Though the long, sharp jaws of *Spinosaurus* were terrifying, it didn't have nearly the bite force of *T. rex.* Like other marine predators of the day, the crocodile-like jaws of *Spinosaurus* were great for grabbing and stabbing slippery fish and holding them steady as they met their demise. But this dino's real lethal weapon was its six-inch (15-cm) sickle-shaped thumb claw, which it used to shred captive prey. *T. rex* had clawless, puny arms, but it had something deadly: 60 serrated eight-inch (20-cm)-long chompers that could crush a car. It was lights out for anything unfortunate enough to have a close encounter.

This epic dino competition wouldn't have been possible without the spectacular science behind every stat and fact in this book. Scientists who study dinosaurs are called paleontolo[gists.] If you want to keep the games going, you c[an] take all you've learned here and make even [] more DinoMania matchups of your own. O[] for gold and become a paleontologist your[] one day! And just maybe this epic battle of[] will keep going for the next 65 million year[s.]

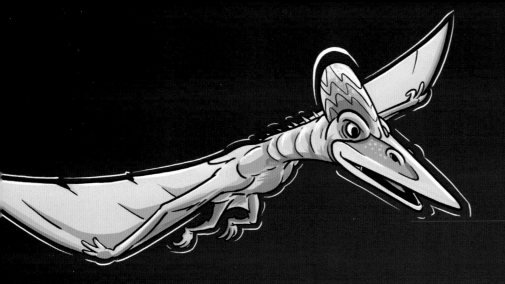

PAW PRINTS PUBLISHING

Copyright © 2024 WonderLab Group LLC

Published by Paw Prints Publishing
A division of Baker & Taylor
Paw Prints Publishing and associated logos are trademarks and/or registered trademarks of Baker & Taylor.

ISBN: 978-1-2231-8866-9 (paperback)
ISBN: 978-1-2231-8865-2 (reinforced library binding)
ISBN: 978-1-2231-8867-6 (e-book)

www.PawPrintsPublishing.com
Printed in China

Created and produced by WonderLab Group LLC

Written by Becky Baines
Illustrated by Daniel Paul
Art direction and design by Fan Works Design LLC
Production design by Project Design Company
Photo research by Annette Kiesow
Expert review by Akiko Shinya
Fact-checked by Jen Agresta
Copyedited by Heather McElwain
Proofread by Molly Reid

Image Credits:

Key: rt=right, le=left, lo=below, bk=background, Shutterstock=Sh

Illustrations by Daniel Paul unless otherwise noted.

Cover: (dinos) Warpaint/Sh, (bk) Net Vector/Sh; Back Cover: (le) Herschel Hoffmeyer/Sh, (lo) Mikael Damkier/Sh; 2, 3 (above), 24 (le): Elenarts/Sh; 3 (lo), 7 (both), 25 (lo rt), 27 (lo): Michael Rosskothen/Sh; 6 (up), 10-11 (Trex, Allo), 14-15 (up), 20 (le), 21 (both), 25 (up le), 27 (up), 28 (Maja), 28-29 (Giga, Trex, Spin), 30 (up): Warpaint/Sh; 6 (lo): QuangTrungArt/Sh; 10 (Orni): YuRi Photolife/Sh; 10 (Dein), 26 (rt): Vac1/Sh; 10 (Velo), 13 (lo rt), 25 (top): Daniel Eskridge/Sh; 10-11 (Troo): Dew_gdragon/Sh; 10-11 (Comp), 14, 15 (lo): Dotted Yeti/Sh; 10 (Orni): Sebastian Kaulitzki/Sh; 11 (top): Four Oaks/Sh; 12 (le), 29 (lo rt), 31 (le): DM7/Sh; 12-13 (lo), 20 (rt), 24 (up): Catmando/Sh; 13 (up le), 28 (Titan), 29 (top), 30 (lo): Herschel Hoffmeyer/Sh; 13 (up rt): Kostiantyn Ivanyshen/Sh; 14-15 (back): Andrei Armiagov/Sh; 15 (rt): Andreas Meyer/Sh; 17: Alberto Andrei Rosu/Sh; 18 (le) Jon Rehg/Sh: 18 (rt): Ginosphotos/Dreamstime; 19 (up): GTS Productions/Sh; 19 (rt): Orchid Lady/Sh; 19 (rt inset): Veronica Krantman/BLM; 19 (lo): Mikael Damkier/Sh; 22 (bk): lmascaretti/Sh; 24 (lo): ChastityQ/Sh; 24 (lo bk): Vector Radiance/Sh; 25 (lo le): Sukjanya/Sh; 25 (rt): Alex Coan/Sh; 26 (le): freestyle images/Sh; 28 (Anky): Innakote/Sh; 30-31 (bk): Net Vector/Sh; 31 (rt): paleontologist natural/Sh